CULTIVATING HUNGER

An Oxfam Study of Food, Power & Poverty

by Nigel Twose

First published in 1984
© Oxfam 1984
Reprinted January 1985

ISBN 0 85598 071 0

Printed by Oxfam Print Unit

Published by Oxfam,
274 Banbury Road,
Oxford, OX2 7DZ
England.

Cover Photo: Nick Fogden

CONTENTS

Cultivating Hunger was published in duplicated form in the autumn of 1984 with the launch of Oxfam's Hungry for Change campaign. It raises a number of issues which Oxfam believes to be crucially related to the imbalances of food production and distribution.

The purpose of the document, and of the campaign, is to call for greater attention to be given to the interests of the poor and the hungry in international policies and negotiations. Further discussion briefs will be issued during 1985 and more detailed studies on some key aspects will be published later.

In view of the encouraging response from the public and the continuing demand for this initial publication, it has been decided to re-issue it in this booklet format.

INTRODUCTION

At the World Food Conference of 1974, the then Secretary of State of the United States, Dr. Henry Kissinger, said:

> *"The profound comment of our era is that for the first time we have the technical capacity to free mankind from the scourge of hunger. Therefore today we must proclaim a bold objective: that within a decade no child will go to bed hungry, that no family will fear for its next day's bread and that no human being's future and capacity will be stunted by malnutrition."*

In fact the number of hungry people has roughly doubled during the decade that Dr. Kissinger referred to, and which has now passed. Over 500 million people — an eighth of humanity — suffer today from chronic malnutrition and the number of hungry people — men, women and children — is increasing year by year. Over 15 million children a year die in infancy from hunger and related causes. This silent holocaust is equivalent to death by starvation of the entire population of London every six months; it is equivalent to the death toll of an Hiroshima explosion every three days. In any circumstances this fact would be an unspeakable tragedy; what transforms it into a moral horror is that — as Dr. Kissinger implied — it need not happen: it could be stopped.

Something has gone terribly wrong with our world food system. More than enough food is being produced to feed the entire population of the planet, but the food is increasingly out of the reach of the poor. The current emphasis on increasing food production is no solution; it's not food that is in short supply, but simple justice.

■ World food supplies are at record high levels. But the food is being grown in the wrong place, and at a price that the world's poor cannot afford.

■ The new systems of crop production which have been introduced into the Third World, for food crops and for export crops,use large quantities of expensive seeds, fertilisers and pesticides which the poor cannot afford. The new systems also need less labour; the poor, excluded by their very poverty, are

5

left to manage as best they can as farmers on the world's most marginal land, or as migrants to city slums.

■ Aid from the rich world for development is being cut back at the very time of greatest need in the poor world. Deprived of adequate investment and assistance in agriculture, poor farmers are obliged to overwork their land in an increasingly vain effort to grow the food they need. Every year an area of once fertile land the size of England and Scotland is lost to production.

■ Poor countries which borrowed money from commercial banks when oil prices rose are unable to repay, now that interest rates have risen so high and the price of the Third World's exports has dropped so low.

■ The International Monetary Fund's strategy for solving the crisis is putting the brunt of the austerity firmly on the shoulders of the poor. One catastrophic consequence has been the acceleration of changes in Third World agricultural practices, resulting in a concentration on crops for export at the expense of food crops for local consumption.

■ Increasing numbers of the poor cannot afford to buy the food which others have produced, and their one lifeline to survival — the food that they grow and eat — has been taken away from them. Instead of food self-sufficiency for all, the new capital-intensive schemes of crop production are helping create market gluts in the rich world.

■ The poor could grow the food that they need, if we could only get the system off their backs. Changes in Third World agricultural policies are certainly necessary, but they can only come about in a significant way if they are preceded by change in the institutions controlled by the rich.

What kind of a world is it that seeks a solution to its sophisticated problems of high finance by taking away food from the poor?

HUNGER MYTHS

While many will acknowledge that there is a problem the explanations of it and solutions to it which they advance are tragically misconceived. The **very myths** that are believed about what causes hunger actually make matters worse and help to perpetuate it. The key thing about these myths is that they enable us to live with the evil of hunger by **transferring responsibility elsewhere** to the poor themselves — by blaming hunger on overpopulation — or to God! by blaming it on the weather.

The weather myth

Many have argued that little can be achieved in the Third World because of the unpredictability of the weather. They point out how a sudden drought or flood can wipe out the annual harvest, leaving families with absolutely no food for the year that stretches ahead of them.

But in fact, the weather in many Third World countries is very good for food production. Traditional agricultural practices represent a long-evolved adaptation to particular features of the tropical climate. Huge numbers of techniques and strategies have been developed over the years to increase the security of food production in the face of uncertain rainfall. For example, seeds may be planted at different times; different varieties of seeds with different maturing times used; or several crops intercropped so that harvests are staggered.

After all, we have had to come to terms with the climate in Britain as well. In this country, we have what could be considered a disaster with our weather every year: it gets so cold that almost nothing will grow for months on end. We call it winter and, knowing that it recurs, we have found ways to cope with it. Just like our winter, many of the Third World's floods and droughts are not the unexpected natural disasters we often imagine. In the Sahel region of West Africa, drought appears to be part of the normal environmental cycle [1]; in parts of Asia, it is known that floods will occur again every year. If these weather extremes are to be expected, then nobody has an excuse for only responding afterwards. They can generally be planned for, so that people will be in a better position to cope.

But even when precautions are taken, the poor remain especially vulnerable simply because of their poverty. Oxfam's Disasters Officer, Marcus Thompson, says: "We are forever attempting to help people who have been forced off the land, piling up in the slums of cities like Bombay or Calcutta. Because of their poverty, they are always more vulnerable to whatever comes along, whether it is a flood, a fire or an epidemic."

The weather does not create disaster for the world's poorest people. The weather does no more than tip the balance for people already living on the brink of survival.

This becomes even clearer when we remember that there has never been a famine in which all sections of the population suffered equally. Different people have very different powers when it comes to acquiring food. Marcus Thompson gives the example of the floods in Calcutta at the beginning of 1984. "A couple of feet of water was a great inconvenience to people living in brick and cement houses, but it didn't destroy the house, and food stocks were just lifted onto the roof out of harm's way. But for people living in a hut, when the rains came they lost the hut and everything in it." In the Sahel, poor farmers on the margins of the Sahara desert are most vulnerable to the inevitable droughts. It's not the fault of the weather but of the forces which push people to the margins of existence. A change in the weather accentuates existing inequalities, pushing some people under while a few actually make a profit from the high prices caused by the food shortages.

So while the drought or flood may be temporary, it has permanent effects for many of the poorest.

Emergency aid efforts often do little more than attempt to help the poorest pick up the pieces, without ever coming to terms with the forces that have taken away their means of survival. It is poverty —not the weather — that is to blame, and it is the relentless pauperisation of those who were already poor that this report will investigate.

The population myth

It is often argued that the poor stay poor because they have too many children. During the summer of 1984, an International Conference on Population in Mexico City drew attention to population growth as a major cause of world hunger. The 1984 World Bank report said much the same thing [2]. But while there is no doubt that the crisis for the poor is compounded by the continuing growth in population, is it fair to say that population growth is itself **causing** the problem?

The world already produces enough food to feed everybody in it. So what do people mean when they talk about 'too many' people? Does 'too many' perhaps relate to the amount of food people eat? Are there too many Americans, because they consume 35% of the world's resources even though they are only 6% of the world's population [3]? The entire population of the Third World uses up only the same quantity of the world's resources as the United States [4].

Or does 'too many' relate to the amount of land available? But Bolivia has 12 people per square mile, Holland has 1,117: so why is there hunger in Bolivia but not in Holland? India has 568 people per square mile, Britain has 583 [5]. Are there too many people in Britain?

If we look at rates of population growth rather than at absolute numbers, then it is no coincidence that rich countries have low rates of population growth and poor countries have high rates. The poor who live off the land have always needed lots of children to help grow the family's food. Even today, many parts of Africa still suffer from shortages of labour at key times of the year, shortages which limit the amount of food which they can produce. In Burkina Faso (formerly Upper Volta), Oxfam field staff visited a leper hospital during the rainy season and found it almost empty: labour shortages are so acute that the severely disabled patients had temporarily discharged themselves to help in the fields.

Poor families in the world's poorest countries never know if their newborn will survive or not, and have always tried to have more children than they actually need just to ensure that some survive. But even when the poor decide that they want fewer children, family planning is often either not available or is too expensive. A comprehensive survey in 1983 showed that 68% of women with four children did not want any more; 39% of women with only two children did not want more [6]. All too often it is **poverty** which is increasing family size.

DEBT:
PRECIPITATING THE CRISIS

In June 1984, the Presidents of six Latin American countries sent a letter to Mrs. Thatcher calling for the London Economic Summit to look at new ways of relieving the poor countries' burden. "An intolerable situation has been reached," they wrote.

To understand the exacerbation of their plight in the last few years, and the hunger crisis facing so many of the poor today, we need to look back to 1973. In October of that year, the price of oil doubled; two months later, it doubled again. These unprecedented increases hit developing countries acutely, and they quickly began to look for loans to help them pay their oil bills. The oil producing countries were meantime generating big financial surpluses; they deposited them with Western banks who had to look for ways to lend the money out again as fast as possible. The result was a startling rush of private bank lending to the Third World.

Money was available quickly, in large amounts, and with few conditions. In his book 'The Money Lenders', Anthony Sampson quotes one Latin American Minister of Finance remembering "how the bankers tried to corner me at conferences, to offer me loans. They wouldn't leave me alone" [7]. Of course, some responsibility must rest with the governments which accepted the loans, but most commentators agree that it was this over-enthusiastic lending by the banks which did more than anything else to precipitate the crisis which was to come.

The money the banks made available completely overshadowed the resources of the World Bank and the International Monetary Fund: responsibility for international financial assistance suddenly shifted into private hands [8].

Banks are commercial institutions which lend for profit. This shift from official to private lending meant that loans were made for a shorter term, and were increasingly made at a floating rate of interest which would adjust to the market rate, rather than being made at a fixed rate. The money was not evenly distributed according to need, but went instead to those countries which the banks assessed could generate sufficient foreign exchange to repay on time.

All the big banks rapidly increased the proportion of profits made abroad. In 1976 alone, Citibank derived 13% of its worldwide earnings from just one country, Brazil [9]. As a general rule, the poorer the country was, the higher the interest and charges [10].

A crisis became inevitable by the late seventies. Recession in industrial countries led to a fall in demand for Third World exports and, in consequence, to an even bigger drop in commodity prices which had been falling continuously for several decades. The price of oil doubled again in 1979 because of supply disruptions in Iran. And the United States budget deficit and high interest rates meant that the dollar began its surge against other currencies. Since more and more of the banks' loans to the poor countries had been made at a floating interest rate, this meant that interest repayments shot upwards.

A few countries — mostly in Latin America — had borrowed so heavily that the only way the banks could avoid immediate disaster was to lend more. Low income countries had borrowed much less in overall cash terms, but the debt often represented a much larger percentage of their national income.

Governments of the powerful industrialised countries were suddenly afraid that the entire international financial system could be under threat if debtor countries declared that they were unable to repay. We shall look at how an attempt to avert this threat has pushed the burden of repayment onto the shoulders of the world's poorest people, thus ensuring that some of the world's richest institutions can continue to make high levels of profit.

AGRICULTURE:
INCREASING PRESSURE FOR CHANGE

In need of foreign exchange for their imports, developing countries have concentrated on producing crops for export since colonial times. Rising import bills (because of inflation in industrialised countries), combined with lower prices paid for their export crops, meant that exports had to be increased. And as countries became more heavily in debt because of the increase in oil prices, they were left no option but to continue to encourage the production of crops for export, even on land where families used to grow their own food.

It is not difficult to increase production of export crops. You pay farmers more for these crops than they would receive if they grew food, and you only offer credit facilities to farmers growing the crops that you want. Farmers respond quickly to such incentives. In Burkina Faso, farmers with a huge millet harvest in the south of the country told Oxfam field staff that they intended to grow more cotton in place of this food crop the following year, because it would be collected by the State at harvest time instead of sitting in their granaries waiting for a buyer. Also, they would receive a guaranteed price for it from the State [11]. Grass roots observations such as these from Africa are paralleled in India: Oxfam's Field Director in Gujarat writes that "richer farmers in many States have increasingly gone for cash crops and neglected food cropping. Here in Gujarat the State is deficient in food production because of this" [12].

Over the last twenty years Africa has doubled its sugar cane output, and tea production has quadrupled [13]. Many of these increases and those of other export crops are due to higher yields, as a result of the intensified research that has been carried out on these crops as opposed to food crops. They are also due to an expansion of the area under cash crops: more than a quarter of the land on which crops are grown in the Third World today is given over to non-food crops. The area of land under soya-bean cultivation in India, primarily for export, increased five times between 1974-1982 [14], while in the Philippines by the end of the seventies one-third of all cultivated land was used to grow food for export rather than for local consumption.

Another significant change in land use has been taking place with

Harvesting millet in Burkina Faso — future years may see this important food crop almost totally replaced by cotton

cattle raising. Between 1960 and 1980, exports of beef cattle from Costa Rica, Guatemala, Honduras and Nicaragua increased more than five times, from 19,570 tons to 110,000 tons [15]. The cattle are raised on grass rather than grain, so the meat is very lean; it is also half the price of similar beef produced in the United States to where most of it is exported. The pressure of the debt crisis means that these beef exports continue to expand, resulting in less and less land being available for food crops.

Beef herd in Central America; exports of beef cattle from Central American countries increased more than five times between 1960 and 1980.

But the sudden increases that were needed to generate sufficient foreign exchange could not be achieved just by changing land use from food crops to export crops; the poor countries also began to turn in increasing numbers to multinational companies, which could supply new technology and expertise. **The new systems of crop production the companies introduced are capital intensive, needing less labour but large quantities of hybrid seeds, fertiliser, and pesticides, almost all of which have to be imported. But the majority of farmers in poor countries are simply not in a position to buy these inputs.**

Export crops such as tea, cotton and tobacco can be very successfully grown on tropical soils. Indeed, cotton has been grown over large areas with yields which are over twice the average yield in the United States [16]. But such crops use up soil nutrients much faster than most food crops. If the nutrients are not replaced with regular supplements of fertilisers, then the soil becomes infertile very quickly. The poor cannot afford to buy the fertilisers, and are not eligible for credit: if they do attempt to grow these crops, they quickly end up with exhausted soils.

Intensification in the level of cropping can only be sustained with a greatly increased use of pesticides. Cotton, now the world's most important non-food crop, covering 5% of the planet's cultivated land area, uses more pesticides than any other crop [17]. When tobacco is grown, vast quantities of pesticides are applied virtually throughout the crop's seven to eight months' growing cycle [18]. Many of these pesticides are dangerous if handled improperly. Indiscriminate use of pesticides can also result in pests developing a resistance to the chemicals, so that the farmer must apply more — and more powerful — pesticides. Even if they are able to afford these expensive imports, poor farmers are unlikely to be able to read the instructions, to be able to afford the protective clothing, or to have had any training in the use of the pesticides. The World Health Organisation estimates that one person in the developing world is poisoned by pesticides every minute of every day. For the richer farmers and landowners, pesticides have brought immediate (though not unqualified) benefits. But these have largely failed to trickle down to the poor [19].

More than half the population of the Third World depend on the land for their livelihood. The majority simply cannot afford imported seeds, fertilisers and pesticides. These capital intensive approaches are generally inappropriate for the majority of farmers, who get trapped into indebtedness as they try to compete. In Brazil, the large sugar cane growers purchase more land from small food growers, who end up as wage labourers on someone else's land, or are forced off the fertile land altogether. Sometimes this has involved brutal evictions.

The system leads inexorably to ever larger farms: in North East Brazil, 9% of landowners now possess more than 80% of the land, with mechanisation resulting in fewer and fewer people employed in full-time agriculture [20]. **The poor have become rapidly poorer, and their one lifeline to survival —the food that they grow and eat — has been taken away from them.**

Spraying tobacco with pesticides in Sri Lanka; vast quantities of pesticides are applied to tobacco throughout its seven to eight month growing cycle.

Food production

While more land continues to be given over to export crops, and research continues to be directed towards increasing production of these crops, per capita production of food crops for local consumption has been falling throughout the Third World.

Maize crop decimated by drought in Kenya.

Africa has suffered a consistent decline in per capita food production since 1970, and the rate of decline is increasing every year. While Zimbabwe had to import 400,000 tonnes of maize in 1984 to feed the population, the Deputy Minister of Agriculture was able to announce a record harvest of tobacco, cotton and soya-beans for export, due primarily, he said, to larger acreages having been planted [21]. Kenya suffered from severe drought in many parts of the country in the same year and, at the time of writing this report, the food harvest looked at great risk. But an Oxfam consultant pointed out that the parts of the country where rainfall almost always remains sufficient are the areas where export crops are grown [22]. These crops are increasingly luxury items for the European market such as strawberries and asparagus.

Today, by far the majority of all developing countries are regular net importers of grain. In 1960, the Third World as a whole imported 20 million tonnes of grain; the figure has now risen to more than 100 million tonnes a year.

Poor countries are doubly caught. While prices for the crops they export have been falling, they are also paying very high prices for their grain imports. The World Bank estimates that in 1981 developing countries paid 10-15% more than the average best market rates for their grain imports: without quick and reliable market information, they were unable to buy at the right moment. This added around three billion dollars to their food bill that year.

Green Revolution: no answer for the poor

Faced with these increasing bills for imported food, many countries worried about local food needs have used the export crop technology for a quick increase in food production for local consumption. This was the so-called Green Revolution, using scientifically developed varieties of wheat, maize and other foodgrains.

The new techniques certainly succeeded in producing more food in India, the Philippines, Mexico and many other countries, and continue to do so today. The new varieties are extremely responsive to fertilisers and have made investment in these inputs very profitable. In fact, crop production rapidly became so profitable that intense competition for land ensued, bringing about even more concentration of property. In many cases — some of them extremely violent — landowners became direct producers themselves, dismissing their tenants and taking the land under direct cultivation. The former tenants have become seasonal wage labourers. In other countries where small farmers have retained access to the land but have lacked capital to buy the inputs, they have sometimes found the new seeds **worse** than their traditional seeds.

The Organisation of Rural Associations for Progress, a partner of Oxfam in Zimbabwe, found that the new varieties only give their best when they are combined with large amounts of fertiliser and water. "Since the majority of our peasant farmers cannot afford the whole package of seed, fertilisers and irrigation, the hybrid seed has tended to yield less than the traditional varieties. Unless the present advocates of hybrid-fertilisers training schemes are prepared to supply better land and irrigation facilities, they have to realise that they are partly responsible for (village families') vulnerability and starvation in times of drought." [23]

Within recent years, for any new variety to be released it needs to yield at least as much as traditional varieties under traditional circumstances. But factors other than yield do not seem to have been given sufficient emphasis.

SR52 is a variety of maize introduced into Southern and East Africa which yields as much as traditional varieties. But the leaves which shield the cob very tightly on the traditional maize do not completely cover it with SR52: as a result, beetles attack and rip the cob to shreds [24].

Almost all the new varieties were only developed to produce higher yields; it is only in the last few years that plant breeders have started to test with regard to cooking, storage and even whether the new variety is actually edible or not.

Although it has become technically possible for those farmers with capital to grow more food, in fact food is not often chosen as a crop. While a rural family with secure use of a piece of land will be likely to grow the food they need before they consider any other crops, the same land in the hands of a landlord will be used to grow whatever is most profitable. This is unlikely to be food for local consumption, since many governments choose to keep food prices as low as possible to satisfy the non-producing but always potentially troublesome urban dwellers. As the cities of the Third World continue to grow, especially in Latin America, this practice has become increasingly expensive and the target of much international criticism.

The World Bank recently encouraged many countries in Africa to increase the price farmers receive for their food crops, as an incentive for them to grow more food. But unlike export crops which are bought by the State or directly by a multinational company, most food crops in Africa are sold on the open market to private traders or to the consumer. This makes official government prices for food mostly irrelevant. And for countries faced with a heavy debt burden, it has been simply impossible to encourage the production of food rather than a crop which will earn foreign exchange.

But even in those countries which have succeeded in growing more food, this has not, in itself, solved the problem of getting food into the mouths of those who need it. In India, the food harvest has increased enormously; the harvest is generally sufficient to meet market needs, yet millions of people are malnourished, unable to afford market prices. Barry Underwood, Oxfam's Field Director in Gujarat, explains:

"The poor farmers and the landless hardly get a look in. They are treated as something separate from the overall 'strategy', and at best they receive some 'bandaid' treatment from Government agencies or other donor agencies" [25]. Oxfam's Field Director in Calcutta, Tony Vaux, concurs: "To service the debt, projects which might conceivably have benefited the poor are cut back, except where other aid sources can be found" [26].

With land and resources in the Third World increasingly devoted to export crops, the poor are being denied the possibility of growing their own food. In global terms, food supplies in the middle of 1983 were at record high levels. But more and more of the poor are unable to buy the food which others have grown. We are forced to conclude that an increase in food production, no matter how great, cannot in itself solve the problem of hunger, which is caused by lack of access to that food or to the resources to produce it.

LOADED DICE:
THE TERMS OF TRADE

It did not take long for the world's poor countries to discover that increased national production of export crops was not going to result in the increase in national income which could have been anticipated. By 1982, world prices for the raw materials exported from the Third World were at their lowest level for fifty years.

Much of the problem is due to the extreme vulnerability which results from concentrating on just a few commodities. Nine countries in Africa are dependent on just one crop for over 70% of their income [27]. 60% of Bangladesh's export earnings come from selling jute or jute products [28]; almost 90% of Burundi's come from coffee [29]. To be so reliant on just one commodity is to be in a very weak bargaining position.

By 1981, it took one Latin American country almost ten times as much beef to buy a barrel of oil as it did in 1973 [30]. Similarly, profits from the export of one tonne of bananas at the end of the seventies were only enough to purchase half as much steel as they bought ten years earlier [31]. Any price rises for individual commodities that occur are patchy and are invariably not sustained.

But while falling prices result in even greater export crop production, with consequent strains on domestic food production, it is price fluctuations which make economic planning a nightmare for the exporting countries. With so many countries being encouraged to produce the same export crops (those which are wanted in the rich countries), it is easy to set them in competition against each other. The result is that companies in rich countries can stop buying from one country temporarily, to force prices down.

One classic example occurred in 1975: the United States bought 100 million dollars' worth of sugar from Brazil but the following year bought none and, instead, increased sugar purchases from the Philippines three times over. In the same two year period, exactly the same thing happened with cotton: the United States purchased 50% less Mexican cotton and 90% less Pakistani cotton than it had the previous year, but bought four times as much Indian cotton [32]. Such

Purchasing power
of developing country exports

1971 — Beef — One barrel of oil

1981 — Beef — One barrel of oil

1970 — Bananas / Profit from 1 tonne — One steel bar

1980 — Bananas / Profit from 1 tonne — Half a steel bar

Source: UNEP

23

practices may keep prices low for the purchaser, but five-year plans become meaningless if a government does not know what its budget is likely to be from one year to the next.

Faced with falling prices and fluctuating markets, even those Third World governments which are concerned by what is happening to the poor in their countries **have** to export even more, if they are not to be even more in debt. Oxfam's former Field Director for coastal West Africa, Wyndham James, reports that Guinea Bissau has seen no option but to ban the sale of peanuts locally, so that the absolute maximum can be exported [33].

But peanuts are a crucial source of protein locally at key times of the year especially for children: their disappearance from markets is likely to have a serious impact on nutrition levels. And what happens to Guinea Bissau's peanuts? Most of them come to Europe to feed our pigs and our cows.

So the poor have been left to fend for themselves, and food production has been left to stagnate — but all for nothing, if national income levels from rising exports are not going to cover the cost of debts and imports.

Photo: Hans Spruÿt

The poor have been left to fend for themselves — with no land, increasing unemployment and ever-rising food prices, millions are forced to scratch a living wherever they can.

AID UNDER ATTACK

The poorest countries with little to export still need to import a variety of products from industrialised countries, as well as increasingly expensive fuel. They are generally not deemed creditworthy by the banks, because they have such a low capacity for generating foreign exchange and have become dependent on foreign aid to finance their development schemes. But at the very moment when their needs were greatest, with inflation pushing up the cost of their imports and with oil prices rising so drastically, the flow of external aid began to fall.

The amount of official development assistance from Western industrialised countries has stagnated since 1980. In 1983, it actually fell 1% from the previous year [34]. Aid from OPEC countries had increased substantially after the oil price rises, but this also fell in 1983 to almost 20% less than the previous year [35]. Only aid from Eastern Europe increased during 1983, but the total figure remains comparatively low when expressed as a percentage of Gross National Product: the Eastern Bloc has never accepted any general responsibility for aid to the Third World.

In the United Kingdom, public spending cuts have hit the budget of the Overseas Development Administration harder than most Government departments. In 1983 the share of our national income going in aid dropped to almost the lowest level for twenty years.

But of course, it is not just the quantity of aid which is significant, but the **quality**. We now know that aid given to one section of the population may directly damage the interests of another, but a large proportion of British aid is still being disbursed without proper appraisal of its impact on the poor. In many cases, too, aid is being used primarily to win export contracts for this country by tying the aid to the purchase of British goods which are not necessarily the most suitable.

The age-old tradition of using aid as political largesse rather than as assistance to the world's poor continues, with particularly tragic examples today. The needs of Ethiopia's 40 million citizens are immense, but the country only received £3.4 million in aid from Britain in 1983 (the same amount as the Seychelles received that year for their population of 60,000).

At the same time as bilateral aid was being cut or increasingly used for political ends, those multinational agencies with the specific objective of helping the poorest countries have been coming under sharp attack, just when the poor are so much in need of assistance. The International Development Association is the soft-loan affiliate of the World Bank, giving interest-free loans over a fifty-year period to the poorest countries; at the start of 1984, the United States reduced its own contribution and — despite an initiative led by Sir Geoffrey Howe — used its political power to persuade other donors to keep the total down.

So even the very poorest countries that were not caught in the banks' debt trap have seen their own development schemes hit by falling levels of aid, while commercial and narrow political considerations have been given even greater priority, at the expense of the relief of poverty. Once again, the needs of the poorest have been largely ignored.

Food Aid: going against the grain

With our grain production increasing so rapidly, it is usually assumed that sending food directly to poorer nations can only do good: after all, what could be more logical than to transfer our market surplus to areas of greater need?

The major problem is that about 70% of all such food aid goes directly to governments, who then sell it to those who can afford to buy it (usually not the poor) and keep the money to supplement their budgets. Some governments have come to rely on these food sales for a significant part of their revenue; it is not in their interests to have agricultural policies which would stimulate greater food production and thereby lose this part of their revenue.

Only 10% of food aid goes to where it is most needed: for emergency relief. The priority given to helping people in these desperate situations is low, and the food often arrives late: when a million Ghanaians were expelled from Nigeria at the start of 1983, Oxfam field staff reported that most people were already back in their villages before the food aid had even arrived in the country. In the summer of 1984, Ethiopia urgently needed 441,000 tonnes of grain to avoid widespread starvation. But at the time of writing this report, only a fraction of the desperately needed relief food had been dispatched.

Oxfam's food aid consultant, Tony Jackson, says that while food aid helps get rid of our own market gluts and can certainly help the poorest at times of emergency, "it doesn't address the basic problem of why food is not being grown where it is needed, and in fact it stops people even considering the issue, by allowing them to think that the problem has been solved".

PASSING THE BUCK:
THE INTERNATIONAL MONETARY FUND

While changes in agriculture — which the Third World had hoped would generate more foreign exchange — were failing to increase revenue sufficiently, the second oil price rise in 1979 was finally enough to persuade the leaders of the rich world that they had to act. Poor countries that were by now hopelessly in debt had not managed to export enough to cover their import needs, as well as repay the commercial loans they had taken out.

Governments from the rich world feared the collapse of the international financial system, but were unwilling to give or lend any more. A summit of Western political leaders held in Venice in 1979 recognised that they had to do something, but decided not to tackle the debt crisis themselves. Instead, they remitted the entire problem to the International Monetary Fund, despite the fact that the IMF was equally inexperienced in dealing with a problem of this kind. But it was the only choice offered to poor countries, who were left with nowhere else to turn.

The IMF's role has traditionally been to help redress short-term balance of payments problems of industrialised countries. It was not established as a development agency, and its staff have consistently denied any responsibility for aiding development [36]. Critics of the decision to involve the IMF argue that if prices for oil and other imports remain high, and prices for export crops remain low, then the Third World's balance of payments is always going to be difficult. Developing countries are not facing the kind of short-term financial hiccough in which the IMF specialises, but a long-term structural problem.

But the poor countries are not just worried about the appropriateness of the IMF's experience. They are equally concerned by the power balance within the structure. All member countries of the IMF are allocated quotas, based on features such as the size of their economies and their participation in world trade. It is this quota which determines a country's voting strength in the Fund. Today, 77% of IMF members are non-oil exporting developing countries, but their voting strength is only 30% [37]. In contrast, the seven nations attending the 1984 Western economic summit in London control 46% of the vote. This means that the policies of the IMF are effectively those of the governments of the rich world.

The IMF does not have anything like the financial reserves necessary to tackle the balance of payments problems facing so much of the Third World. But a solution of sorts was found: commercial banks stopped all loans to developing countries unless they adopted an IMF programme of adjustment to the economy, and obtained the Fund's seal of approval. The IMF refers to this as "the catalytic effect the Fund can have in helping to unlock additional finance from other external creditors" [38].

Since 1983, any increase in commercial bank lending to the Third World has been almost entirely due to rescheduling of existing debt, under the auspices of IMF agreements. Ghana's Finance and Planning Secretary, Dr Kwesi Botchway, recently stated that Ghana could not find help anywhere until it went to the IMF: they had been left "no realistic alternative" [39].

But when we begin to look at the economic adjustment programmes which the IMF has introduced into the Third World, it quickly becomes clear that their solution for the debt crisis is no different from their solution for short-term hiccoughs in rich countries. Their adjustment programmes aim to reduce expenditure and at the same time to build up the productive base of the economy [40]. But when the starting point is a very low level of income for the poor, then any austerity measures risk catastrophic consequences for those at the bottom of the pile.

Adjustment programmes generally include, in part, import reductions which lead to reduced economic activity and higher unemployment. They also include credit ceilings being imposed on both the public and the private sectors [41]; in the short term, at least, this increases unemployment and reduces real wages. Government expenditure is reduced, and the targets of such cuts are invariably the social services and food subsidies. IMF staff accept that their programmes are unlikely to be 'distributionally neutral' [42], and it is the poor who are least able to protect themselves against such cuts. Third World countries have no welfare state and, for those millions of families already living below the poverty line, the IMF's lack of 'distributional neutrality' does not just mean temporary discomfort. It means hunger, often with permanent effects.

But it is not just the austerity measures which affect the poor. **As far**

as food needs are concerned, the major result of an IMF intervention in the Third World is the acceleration of changes in agricultural practices, resulting in even greater concentration on crops for export, at the expense of food crops for local consumption.

Clearly, the economists in Washington and the governments of the rich world which decide the policies of the IMF do not believe that there is a structural problem. Abysmal terms of trade do not seem to concern them. It was not until September 1984 that an IMF annual report made a point of criticising the effect of the US budget deficit and the resultant high interest rates. In the same month, the World Bank added its powerful voice to the growing body of criticism of the present handling of the debt crisis. Can it be right for the world's poorest people to be asked to tighten their belts even more? We shall look at some effects of the IMF's programme in the next chapter.

FULL FIELDS BUT EMPTY STOMACHS

It does not look as if the IMF 'solution' of increasing exports even more will ever be able to counterbalance the effects of appalling terms of trade and high interest rates. But even if it could succeed, it is still legitimate to ask: **can it be right to make the world's poorest people pay for a crisis that they had no part in creating?**

Despite public lip-service to food self-sufficiency, national food strategies in the Third World are left to one side, and agricultural production is geared to generating foreign exchange. The poor are left to manage as best they can on already vulnerable and poor quality land on which export crops cannot be grown. They struggle every year to produce enough food to feed themselves and their families, but more and more of them are failing to do so.

They are forced to take more from the soil than they should, while not possessing the resources to put back the necessary nutrients with manure or chemical fertilisers. The land is not being allowed time to regenerate, and the protective top cover is not being restored. Water and wind erosion gradually thin the topsoil, and **every year** 80,000 square miles (the area of England and Scotland combined) of once fertile land declines to a point where it will no longer yield anything [43].

Migration: the final solution

On arid land along the edge of deserts like the African Sahara, poor farmers have no choice left to them but to encroach onto the traditional land of the pastoralists. Their flexible grazing system is based on tracking down pockets of good pasture created by localised showers; they need access to large areas of this marginal land for their system to work. But, compressed onto ever smaller areas, the crucial flexibility of their system has been limited and, with it, their ability to withstand erratic rainfall or drought. As more and more of the poor are left with no choice but to attempt to grow their food on marginal arid land, the pastoralists' system becomes less and less workable [44].

Every year, 80,000 square miles of once fertile land declines to a point where it will no longer yield anything.

In other parts of the world, poor farmers have begun to exploit tropical forests in a manner that simply cannot be sustained. This has been going on for decades, but now governments are searching for places to relocate the poor for whom there is no longer any room on the fertile land, and are actively promoting the migration of impoverished peasants into lowland forest zones. Small-scale farming has become the major factor in the destruction of the world's forests. As ever larger numbers of peasants have been pushed into the forests by circumstances beyond their control, less forest land is available; the system the farmers practise becomes more intensive, the soil becomes exhausted and quickly degenerates into scrub. In the Philippines alone, over 2,000 square miles of forest are permanently abandoned every year after the soil has been exhausted beyond recovery. The Food and Agriculture Organisation estimates that more than 43,000 square miles of forest worldwide are being cleared each year to make way for agriculture. Tropical forests harbour more than two-fifths of the world's plants and animal species, they contain four-fifths of the world's land vegetation; they help regulate the climate, and they keep rivers running throughout the year. But with growing pressures on them, they look likely to be all but destroyed within the lifetime of our children [45].

Small-scale farming has become the major factor in the destruction of the world's forests.

Other farmers who cannot participate in cash crop production because of their poverty take the road which leads to the city. The world's largest urban areas are increasingly in the Third World, where cities are growing at almost twice the rate of overall populations. London, which was the world's second largest city as recently as 1950, will not even rank among the 25 largest by the end of the century [46]. Over half of the population of Latin America are now urban dwellers [47], as are 38% of Zaire's and Egypt's populations. Once in the cities, the poor may still look for seasonal work on nearby agricultural land; they may find other low wage labour; they may remain unemployed; or they may send their children out to work. The number of children who make their living on Brazil's city streets has risen 90% in the last three years, to more than 30 million [48]. The huge number of urban poor no longer growing their own food creates an additional burden on national food production which must now make some attempt to feed these people. In 1978, a survey of Latin American cities showed that 60% of the expenditure of households in the lowest income categories went on food and beverages [49]. Such a high percentage of an already minimal income makes the poor especially vulnerable to the sorts of price rises which the IMF has encouraged, making it ever more difficult for them to get the food which their families need.

In the 1960s the predominant development philosophy was the 'trickle down' theory: wealth injected into a country, stimulating economic growth, would eventually trickle down to the poorest. Most observers now agree that this 'trickle down' of wealth simply hasn't worked — the poor on the whole do not benefit from development achievements. Oxfam's Campaign Manager, John Clark, points out: "What we're witnessing today is the successful working of another type of 'trickle down', the trickle down of poverty. Through the IMF austerity conditions, through a transfer from food to export crops, through spiralling food prices and plummeting wages, the impact of the debt crisis is successfully trickling down to the poorest of the poor".

The poor may not have benefited from development efforts; they didn't create the debt crisis, but now they are paying for it.

Predictable ill health

Actual starvation is still rare in the world, even among children, but it is estimated that 500 million people are suffering from malnutrition, a

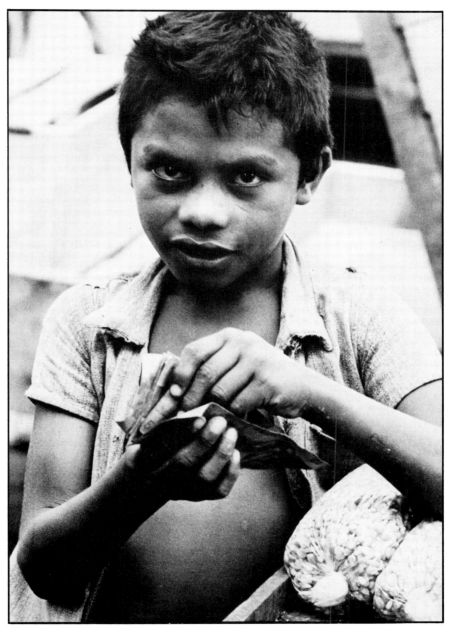

The number of children who make their living on Brazil's city streets has risen to more than 30 million in the last three years.

lack of calories [50]. It is not a question of people eating the 'wrong' food. The poor just do not have enough to eat.

Such shortages affect children most acutely, since a young child needs twice as much protein and three times as many calories as an adult, per kilo of body weight [51]. This lack of food increases both the frequency and the severity of disease: children with even moderate malnutrition are three times more likely to contract diarrhoeal infections, and up to ten times more likely to die from simple diseases like measles. 97% of the world's infant deaths (that is, under 1 year) and 98% of the world's child deaths (1-4 years) occur in the Third World [52].

Commenting on these quite unnecessary levels of sickness and death, an Indian magazine declares its belief that we are already in the middle of the Third World War: "A war waged in peacetime, without precedent, and involving the largest number of deaths and the largest number of soldiers without uniform" [53].

Reaction

What kind of world is it that seeks a solution to its sophisticated problems of high finance by taking away food from the poor? Less and less land is available for food production in the Third World; little investment is made to increase food crop yields in the countries where food is most needed; food prices are rising; wages are falling. Who can blame the poor if they object? They are being made to pay the price of a crisis which they had no part in creating.

Oxfam offices in Latin America are reporting dramatic stories about the reaction of the poor to this imposed hunger: food riots resulting in 60 deaths in the Dominican Republic; crowds of hungry people raiding supermarkets at night in Brazil; street demonstrations and marches in Mexico; food riots in Haiti. With traditional means of survival being taken away from the poor, their reaction is not surprising: what was once a struggle for justice and a fairer distribution of food, land and power is increasingly becoming a fight for survival.

Many governments are responding with repression. The Third World is currently importing nearly 25 billion dollars' worth of armaments from the major industrialised countries [54]. Increasing proportions of the weapons and technologies they are importing are designed to control hungry and angry citizens: riot weapons, crowd monitoring equipment, computerised intelligence networks, prison and torture equipment [55].

World arms exports are dominated by sales from the USA and USSR, but the leading suppliers of this specialised repressive technology are the United States and Britain. 350 people are employed at the Ministry of Defence to sell our weapons. 77% of British arms exports are to the Third World [56], and it is a British company which holds the dubious distinction of having been the first to develop a vehicle specifically to 'deter' riots: the AMAC-1 has nineteen weapon points, four multiple grenade launchers, a water cannon, an infra-red video camera for surveillance, and its body-work can be electrified with a 7,000 volt charge. It was advertised by its makers early in 1984 as "the ultimate riot deterrent" [57].

Twenty-five countries which have had to reschedule their foreign debts since 1981 spent 11 billion dollars in the preceding five years on equipment like this to repress their own hungry citizens [58].

Photo: Mike Goldwater, Network

Many governments are responding with repression. Since 1976 approximately 35,000 people have disappeared in Guatemala, which Amnesty International has accused of being the most consistent and brutal violator of human rights in Latin America.

THE NEED FOR CHANGE

It is important to remember that these are complex issues: there are no simple solutions. Nonetheless, 500 million people — the equivalent of the total population of Europe — are being denied one of the most basic human needs: food. For any change to take place, we must first recognise that it is the present system of world food production and distribution which is failing disastrously.

The world's poor are being brought into a world food system in which the crude power of economic forces prevails over all moral considerations. All that the poor are offered is food grown elsewhere at a price they cannot afford. **The poor could grow the food they need, if we could only get the system off their backs**. Instead, our taxes continue to subsidise the market gluts of the rich world.

It appears that governments of the world's rich countries are unwilling to negotiate meaningfully on the key issues which would allow governments of the poor to work towards food self-sufficiency for all. Without change in the world trade system, producers will never get a fair return for their commodities. Without change in the terms of loan repayments, the poor's food supply will remain in jeopardy. Without change in aid programmes, smaller farmers' attempts to grow their own food will become increasingly unsuccessful. And without change in the agricultural policies of the rich world, poor countries will continue to be encouraged to produce more and more export crops to help us create market gluts.

This report has concentrated on the need for change in the institutions controlled by the rich. But, were such changes to take place, then it would be up to Third World governments to institute parallel changes in their agricultural policies. Agrarian reform based on the needs of the poor. Pricing strategies that would encourage food production. Greater access to agricultural credit and inputs for the poor. More research on food production. And more resources for the redistribution of grain harvests from surplus areas of a country to deficit communities. Such moves are essential, but can only come about in a significant way if they are preceded by change in the rich. It's our decision.

THE CHALLENGE FOR BRITAIN

In this report we identify five main areas, five forces, by which we in Britain in particular are connected with the Crisis of Hunger. We are not suggesting that this is a complete list, but we are convinced that these areas need special and urgent attention.

Oxfam does not have the answers. We do not know exactly how the institutions and policies should be reformed to lessen the oppression of poverty, but we are certain that, through these five forces, our society is contributing to the creation and maintenance of hunger in the world and that this is morally indefensible.

Of course, Oxfam and other organisations have put forward — and will continue to do so — arguments for reform, calls for change. There are a number of campaigns relating to these proposals. We are suggesting here some new initiatives, and some strengthening of existing calls.

The five areas of focus are:

Debt

Removing the burden of the debt crisis and crippling interest rates from the shoulders of the very poor.

In particular —

— Removing IMF austerity conditions which lead to the poor having even less food.
— Protecting poor countries from fiercely crippling interest charges.
— Reforming the international financial institutions (especially the IMF) or, if this is not feasible, creating new structures that can cope sensitively with the crisis of poverty.

Aid

Renewing the imperative for official Government aid: that it should be a powerful weapon in the fight against poverty and hunger in the world and not an instrument for furthering our political and commercial self-interests.

In particular —

— Increasing the level of appropriate Government aid.
— Targeting a much greater proportion of this aid to the direct needs of the poor and especially to the fundamental problem of fighting hunger.
— Reforming food aid so that it is more freely available when needed in times of emergency or special needs, but so that it does not interfere with the production and distribution of basic food needs in developing countries.
— Giving paramount consideration to social issues (particularly the impact on women and children) and to environmental factors in the planning of any aid project.

Trade

Improving the terms of trade so that the poor are no longer exploited in the world market place.

In particular —

— Setting up commodity agreements that ensure reasonable prices for Third World commodities.
— Supporting mechanisms that limit the drift towards more and more export crop production, and greater competition between developing countries.
— Contributing to the establishment of clear and binding ethical codes governing the operations of international companies, particularly in the fields of food and commodity production and marketing.
— Reducing the barriers to trade with developing countries (especially in processed and semi-processed commodities).

Agricultural Policies of the North

Reforming our agricultural system so that it is no longer so wasteful and so draining on the world's food and such a heavy burden on the hungry.

In particular —

— Increasing self-sufficiency by using land to grow Europe's needs, not food that is destroyed or wastefully used to feed animals.

— Reducing dependency on exotic animal feeds such as soya from Brazil, groundnuts from West Africa, cassava from Thailand and anchovies from Peru. These feeds contribute to growing surpluses and drain nutritious foods from developing countries.
— Ending the dumping of sugar and other commodities on the world market, depressing world prices of commodities on which trade poor countries may depend.

Arms Trade

Encouraging a transfer of spending from the Arms Race to Development.

In particular —

— Cutting out Government encouragement for arms-dealing with the Third World (e.g. through the Defence Sales Organisation and export fairs).
— Carefully restricting the export of repressive arms and equipment likely to be used for quelling internal disturbance caused by the anger of the hungry.

Ten years from now, no child NEED go to bed hungry. No family SHOULD have to fear for the next day's bread. But will they?

A CASE STUDY: BRAZIL

Brazil is one of the largest food exporters in the world, yet the country has huge levels of malnutrition. One Oxfam survey in Ceara State showed that about half the children under five were malnourished [59]. Another survey described 70% malnutrition in North East Brazil. Some areas report 25% infant mortality rates.

It would be easy to say that these unprecedented levels of hunger are caused by drought, but if we look a little closer we see how simplistic that would be. North East Brazil seems to experience a drought every 7-10 years; the impact of this one is different for several inter-related reasons:

■ The debt crisis has gripped. While interest rates were lower, the Brazilian Government felt able to make the repayments, but as US prime rates shot higher and higher it became impossible for Brazil to pay the interest charges without massive changes in its economy.

■ In order to reschedule its debts, the Brazilian Government negotiated with the IMF. The terms of the agreement included swingeing austerity measures. The largest package, agreed in June 1983, chopped more than 2 billion dollars off government spending, and ended the indexing of wages to cost-of-living [60]. The wages of the poor (that is, those lucky enough to have jobs) started to plummet.

■ Hyper-inflation ensures that the poor pay a disproportionate share of the debt crisis, even though they were never the beneficiaries of loans in the first place. In a twelve-month period food prices rose 310%, while wages rose just 175% [61]. Millions of the poor can no longer afford to buy staple foods like beans and rice.

■ There is a rapid shift in land use from growing local food to growing cash crops for export. The acreage of land growing oranges has increased by 6% over the last two years; in contrast the amount of land under maize has decreased by almost 6% since 1981, and land under rice has decreased 10% during the same period [62]. In addition, there has been the enormous Gasohol programme where sugar cane is converted into alcohol to fuel cars, in an attempt to cut petroleum imports (about two-thirds of Brazilian cars now run on alcohol). 1984's trade surplus will be double the previous year's, but the savings will all be swallowed up by interest repayments on debts.

These are the factors which have really hit the poor. The wealthiest 20% of the population of Brazil now has an income that is 33 times greater than that of the poorest 20% — the widest income disparity of any country in the world [63]. Even larger numbers of poor farmers and farm labourers are being squeezed off the land, and are flocking to shanty towns outside the sprawling cities. Their food situation is getting desperate. Mothers are forming together in gangs and, rather than see their children starve, they are looting supermarkets for food. São Paulo sees one such raid every night. Some parents, unable to provide food, are abandoning their small children to die.

The Growing Burden of Brazil's Foreign Debt

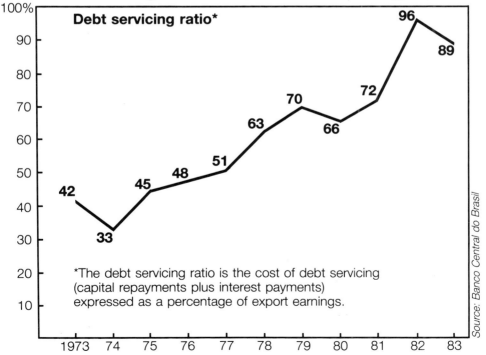

Debt servicing ratio*

*The debt servicing ratio is the cost of debt servicing (capital repayments plus interest payments) expressed as a percentage of export earnings.

Source: Banco Central do Brasil

Notes and References

1. Nigel Twose, *'Drought and the Sahel: why the poor suffer most'*, Oxfam 1984.
2. *'World Development Report 1984'*, World Bank, Oxford University Press 1984.
3. Susan George and Nigel Paige, *'Food for Beginners'*, Writers and Readers 1982, P.68.
4. Ibid.
5. Ibid.
6. *'Population Misconceptions'*, Population Concern 1984.
7. Anthony Sampson, *'The Money Lenders'*, Hodder & Stoughton 1981.
8. Ibid.
9. Ibid.
10. The banks claimed that their risks were higher.
11. Nigel Twose, *'Drought and the Sahel'*, op.cit.
12. Personal correspondence, July 1984.
13. Calculated from FAO production yearbooks.
14. Ibid.
15. Calculated from Norman Myers' *'The Primary Source'*, Norton 1984, P.132.
    Since the 1979 revolution in Nicaragua, cattle exports have dropped markedly and food production has increased.
16. R. Goodland, C. Watson and G. Ledec, *'Environmental Management in Tropical Agriculture'*, Westview Press 1984.
17. Ibid.
18. Ibid.
19. David Bull, *'A Growing Problem'*, Oxfam 1982.
20. *'An Unnatural Disaster: drought in North East Brazil'*, Oxfam 1984.
21. Zimbabwe Herald, 25.7.84.
22. Internal Oxfam report by Brian Hartley, June 1984.
23. ORAP development seminar background paper, April 1984.
24. Personal correspondence from grain storage consultant John Rowley, August 1984.
25. Personal correspondence, July 1984.
26. Personal correspondence, July 1984.
27. Calculated from FAO trade yearbooks, and Economist Intelligence Unit quarterly reports.
28. Ibid.
29. Personal correspondence from Oxfam Field Director for Burundi, Whitney Garberson, August 1984.
30. *'The State of the Environment 1984'*, United Nations Environment Programme, Nairobi 1984.
31. Ibid.
32 Susan George, *'Feeding the Few'*, Institute for Policy Studies 1978, P.10.
33. Personal correspondence, September 1984.
34. *'World Development Report 1984'*, op.cit.
35. Organisation for Economic Cooperation and Development, *'West Africa'* magazine, 2.7.84.
36. Graham Bird, *'The International Monetary System and the Less Developed Countries'*, Macmillan 1982, P.11.
37. Tony Killick, *'The Quest for Economic Stabilisation'*, Heinemann/ODI 1984.
38. J. de Larosière, *'Current Policies of the IMF: Fact and Fiction'*, IMF, Washington, 1983, P.5.
39. Interviewed in *'South'* magazine, July 1984.

40. Tony Killick, op.cit.
41. Ibid.
42. Ibid.
43. Alan Grainger *'Desertification'*, Earthscan 1982, P.9.
44. Nigel Twose, *'Drought and the Sahel'*, op.cit.
45. This paragraph is drawn from Norman Myers' *'The Primary Source'*, op.cit. Chapter 8.
46. *'World Development Report 1984'*, World Bank, op.cit.
47. Ibid.
48. Figures from a study by juvenile authorities in Salvador, quoted in The Guardian, 26.7.84.
49. Philip Musgrove, *'Consumer Behaviour in Latin America: Income and Spending in Ten Andean Cities'*, Brookings Institution, Washington, 1978.
50. FAO.
51. UNICEF, *'The State of the World's Children 1984'*, Oxford University Press 1983.
52. Ibid.
53. *'Illustrated Weekly'*, of India, 3.6.84.
54. *'World Military and Social Expenditure 1983'*, World Priorities, Washington, 1983.
55. Steve Wright, *'The Export of Repressive Technology'*, Richardson Institute for Conflict and Peace Research, University of Lancaster 1984.
56. *'World Armaments and Disarmaments'*, Stockholm International Peace Research Institute, 1984.
57. Information from the Campaign Against the Arms Trade.
58. *'World Military and Social Expenditures 1983'*, op.cit.
59. *'An Unnatural Disaster'*, op.cit.
60. *'Aid is Not Enough'*, Independent Group on British Aid 1984.
61. The Guardian, 24.2.84.
62. Calculated from FAO production yearbooks and Economist Intelligence Unit quarterly reports.
63. *'Geo'* magazine (USA), September 1984, P.144.

Further Reading

FOOD

Food for Beginners: George, S. and Paige, N. Writers and Readers Collective, London.
Food First: Moore Lappé, F. and Collins, J. Souvenir Press, London.
Against the Grain — the dilemma of project food aid: Jackson, T. and Eade, D. Oxfam 1982.
Food Poverty and Power: Buchanan. Russell Press, Nottingham, 1983.
Feeding the Few: George, S.Pelican.
How the Other Half Dies: George, S. Institute for Policy Studies, (available from Third World Publications, Birmingham.)
Seeds of Plenty, Seeds of Want: Pearse, A. Clarendon Press, Oxford, 1980.
Poverty and Famines — an essay on entitlement and deprivation: Amartya Sen. Clarendon Press, Oxford, 1981.

NORTH-SOUTH

Brandt Report I: North-South — a Programme for Survival: Brandt Commission, Pan 1980.
Brandt Report 2: Common Crisis — Co-operation for World Recovery: Brandt Commission, Pan 1983.
The Brandt Report Study Pack. Oxfam 1980.

IMF

The Quest for Economic Stabilisation: ed. Killick, T. ODI/Heinemann 1984.
The Poverty Brokers: Latin America Bureau 1983.
No to Recession and Unemployment — an examination of the Brazilian economic crisis: Furtado, C. Third World Foundation for Social and Economic Studies 1984.

ENVIRONMENTAL IMPLICATIONS

Down to Earth: Eckholm, E. Pluto Press1982.
Desertification: Grainger. Earthscan 1982.
A Growing Problem — pesticides and the Third World poor: Bull, D. Oxfam 1982.

WEATHER

An Unnatural Disaster: Drought in North East Brazil. Oxfam 1984.
Lessons to be Learned: Drought and Famine in Ethiopia. Oxfam 1984.
Why the Poor Suffer Most: Drought and the Sahel. Oxfam 1984.
Disasters and Development: Cuny, F. Oxford University Press 1983.

AID

Real Aid: A Strategy for Britain. Independent Group on British Aid 1982. Available from Oxfam, Christian Aid, World Development Movement, ODI.
Aid is Not Enough: Britain and the World's Poor. Independent Group on British Aid 1982. Available as above.
British Overseas Aid 1983: Overseas Development Administration. HMSO 1984.

HEALTH

The State of the World's Children. UNICEF/Oxford University Press 1984.

ARMAMENTS

World Military and Social Expenditures: World Priorities. Available from Campaign Against the Arms Trade.

BANKS

The Money Lenders: Sampson, A. Hodder & Stoughton 1981.

HUNGRY FOR CHANGE
OXFAM'S CAMPAIGN FOR JUSTICE NOT HUNGER

Oct. 10th 1984 saw the beginning of Oxfam's major new national Campaign, **Hungry for Change.** It is a Campaign about Food and Hunger, but more than that it's a Campaign about the world food system which is so obviously failing the hundreds of millions of people who go hungry. It is a Campaign which believes in the power of ordinary people in the rich developed countries to help change that system to the benefit of the poor.

Hungry for Change offers a great challenge and a great promise: that if you and enough people like you make a stand against this gross injustice, real change will happen — the poor will have more food. From small beginnings, groups of 10 or 20 in each town, Oxfam intends to build a movement of 1 million people active and vocal in the call for change.

STARTING POINTS
Declare your support — **now**

- Find out more about the Campaign
- Join the debate about poverty and hunger
- Organise your local **Hungry for Change** Group, work together and pass your feeling of commitment to others
- Arrange **Hungry for Change** meetings to see slide sets and video films
- Take the Campaign out to other people by helping with the **Hungry for Change** survey

For further details of these and all local Campaign events and for supporting materials please contact your local Oxfam Office (address in telephone directory) or write for details to:

The Campaigns Unit
Oxfam House
274 Banbury Road
Oxford OX2 7DZ
England